THE
BEST
WORST
DAD
JOKES

Other Books by Sandy Silverthorne

Crack Yourself Up Jokes for Kids

More Crack Yourself Up Jokes for Kids

Made You Laugh!

Now That's Funny

THE BEST WORST DAD JOKES

All the Puns, Quips, and Wisecracks
You Need to Torment Your Kids

Sandy Silverthorne

Revell

a division of Baker Publishing Group
Grand Rapids, Michigan

© 2022 by Sandy Silverthorne

Published by Revell
a division of Baker Publishing Group
PO Box 6287, Grand Rapids, MI 49516-6287
www.revellbooks.com

Printed in the United States of America

Library of Congress Cataloging-in-Publication Data
Names: Silverthorne, Sandy, 1951– author.
Title: The best worst dad jokes : all the puns, quips, and wisecracks you need to
    torment your kids / Sandy Silverthorne.
Description: Grand Rapids, MI : Revell, a division of Baker Publishing Group,
    [2022]
Identifiers: LCCN 2021045642 | ISBN 9780800741945 (casebound) | ISBN
    9780800740337 (paperback) | ISBN 9781493436392 (ebook)
Subjects: LCSH: Wit and humor, Juvenile. | LCGFT: Humor.
Classification: LCC PN6166 .S565 2022 | DDC 818/.60208—dc23
LC record available at https://lccn.loc.gov/2021045642

The author is represented by WordServe Literary Group, www.wordserveliterary
.com.

Baker Publishing Group publications use paper produced from sustainable forestry
practices and post-consumer waste whenever possible.

22   23   24   25   26   27   28   7   6   5   4   3   2   1

To my dad, Jack Silverthorne,
the original dad jokester in my life:
Thanks for giving me your sense of humor
and a ton of art supplies.

To Vicki, one half of my dad joke audience:
Thank you for your love, support, and laughter.
You are truly a gift from God.
It's an adventure doing life with you.

To Christy, the other half of my audience
and sometime contributor:
Thanks for being an amazing example
of someone who loves God and loves people.

And special thanks to Todd and Steve
from LIFE 100.3's *Get-Up & Go Show*.
You guys "see the funny" and bring bad dad jokes
every morning on Ontario's Christian Superstation.

Warning: This book might be hazardous if it ends up in the wrong hands.

Like the hands of a dad, stepdad, grandpa, uncle, faux pa (a guy with no kids), or even a teacher, pastor, or the guy in the cubicle next to you at work. And at no time whatsoever must this book be used to torment family members, friends, or coworkers.

The Best Worst Dad Jokes joke book is full of genuinely eye-rolling one-liners like these:

A store owner fought off a robber using only his labeling gun. Police are now looking for a man with a price on his head.

There was a time when I couldn't pay the electric bill. It was the darkest time in my life.

So, if you're a dad who just received this book—be careful. As tempting as it may be, don't in any case afflict your children with lines like the following:

I burnt my Hawaiian pizza. I guess I should have put it on aloha temperature.

What do you call a hippie's wife?
Mississippi.

Oh, okay, go ahead and torment, torture, or flabbergast your entire family with these amazing jokes, riddles, and one-liners. And many years from now, when your kids are older, they'll look back with fondness and cherish the moments when dad shared these hilarious anecdotes with them. Or they'll move to Nebraska and forget the whole thing.

Instructions

1. Read a joke in this award-seeking book.
2. Find an unsuspecting person. It's especially helpful if they're a member of your family.
3. Share the hilarious line.
4. If there's no response, slow down and repeat the joke, followed by the words "Get it?"
5. If there's still no response, slowly explain the joke to the listener. This always increases the enjoyment of the listener and the effectiveness of the humor.

So, get going! Be the bearer of hilarious dad jokes wherever you go.

I named my dogs Rolex and Timex. They're my watch dogs.

Kid: Have you seen my sunglasses?
Dad: No, have you seen my dad glasses?

The first French fries weren't really cooked in France. They were cooked in Greece.

Did you hear about the guy who invented Tic Tacs? They say he made a mint.

I'm reading a book on antigravity. I can't put it down.

I told my wife to embrace her mistakes. She came over and gave me a hug.

Dad: Son, I got you a dictionary for your birthday.

Kid: Gee thanks, Dad. I don't know what to say.

Dad: I know. That's why I got it for you.

Dad: Did you hear about the two guys who stole a calendar?

Daughter: Please, Dad, no . . .

Dad: They each got six months.

Here are the three unwritten rules of life:
1.
2.
3.

What's a foot's favorite snack?
Dori-toes.

No matter how much you push the envelope, it's still stationary.

What do you call a factory that makes average stuff?
A satis-factory.

What do you call a lonely cheese?
Prov-alone.

Sorry about your wait.

Are you saying I'm fat?

Son: Dad, what is irony?
Dad: The opposite of wrinkly.

I opened my shoe store for only large-sized shoes. It was no small feat.

Why do melons have weddings?
'Cause they cantaloupe!

What's the leading cause of dry skin?
Towels.

Kid: My dad's a kleptomaniac.
Friend: Is he taking anything for it?

A slice of apple pie costs $2.50 in Jamaica and $3.25 in the Bahamas. These are the pie rates of the Caribbean.

I needed a password eight characters long. So I chose *Snow White and the Seven Dwarfs*.

DAD QUOTE: I don't have a dad bod; I have a father figure.

Did you hear about the policeman who opened a gardening service?
He called it Lawn Order.

Why did the school put their cafeteria on the second floor?
They wanted to take lunch to the next level.

DAD QUOTE: There was a time when I couldn't pay the electric bill. It was the darkest time in my life.

Where do post office workers go on vacation?
Parcel-ona.

Guy: I tried to make a date with the librarian.
Friend: What happened?
Guy: She was already booked.

Got hit with a bottle of omega-3 tablets yesterday. I'm okay. My injuries were super fish oil.

RANDOM THOUGHTS

My fear of moving stairs is escalating.

I love my fingers; I can always count on them.

Someone stole my lamp. Now I'm delighted.

Dad: Look at that flock of cows over there.

Daughter: Herd of cows.

Dad: Of course I've heard of cows. There's a
whole flock of them over there.

And look at this! It's near schools!

I childproofed my house, but the kids still figured out how to get in.

Where does a cakemaker grow up?
Bakersfield.

What do you call a fish with two knees?
A two-knee fish!

Why did the scarecrow win an award?
Because he was out standing in his field.

Why did the clock get kicked out of class?
It tocked too much.

I went to the air and space museum. There was nothing there.

Dad: Why did the invisible man turn down the job offer?

Kid: I don't want to know.

Dad: He just couldn't see himself doing it.

Did you hear the joke about quicksand?

It takes a long time to sink in.

Why does the composer work in bed?
He's composing sheet music.

What do you call an empty can of Cheez Whiz?
Cheese was.

How do you stay warm in any room?
Go to the corner—it's always 90 degrees.

There's a brand-new kind of broom. It's sweeping the nation!

Do you think jellyfish are sad that there are no peanut butter fish?

My friend likes to take the elevator, but I like to take the escalator. I guess we were raised differently.

Your mom didn't think I could build a car out of spaghetti. You should have seen her face when I drove pasta.

What do you call a pup living in Alaska?
A chilly dog.

What do ants get when they finish all their chores?
Their allow-ants.

I called the tinnitus helpline. It just kept ringing.

I hired a limousine, but the driver never showed up. I paid all that money and had nothing to chauffeur it.

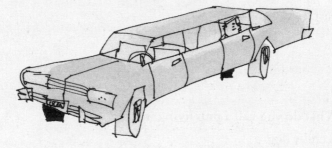

I'm anxious about starting my new job at the restaurant. I can't wait.

Dad: Did you hear about my new groundbreaking invention?

Son: No, what is it?

Dad: A shovel.

RANDOM THOUGHTS

Whenever I try to eat healthy, a chocolate
bar looks at me and Snickers.

I'm giving away my broken guitar.
No strings attached.

I for one like Roman numerals.

People think I'm a good singer. They tell me
I should sing solo. Solo they can't hear me.

Or they think I should sing tenor.
Tenor twelve miles away from here.

If you turn a canoe over, you can wear it as a hat.
That's because it's cap-sized.

When I'm hungry for candy at work, it's never a problem 'cause I always have a few Twix up my sleeve.

DAD QUOTE: I tell dad jokes, but I have no kids. Guess I'm a faux pa!

I know a lot of jokes about retired people—but none of them work.

What do Santa's elves listen to as they work?
Wrap music!

The optimist says the glass is half full. The pessimist says the glass is half empty. The mom says, "Why didn't you use a coaster?"

What do you call a hippie's wife?
Mississippi.

I'm always suspicious of trees on sunny days. Maybe it's just me, but they seem shady.

What do you call a fake noodle?
An impasta!

RANDOM THOUGHTS

I burned 2,000 calories today. I left my dinner in the oven too long.

I never buy anything made of Velcro. It's a total rip-off.

If you want to get a job at a moisturizer factory, you have to apply daily.

What movie mogul works in a bank?
Vault Disney.

Dad: Why are you taking those crackers into the
classroom?
Kid: It's parrot-teacher conference day.

What do you call two guys hanging on a window?
Kurt and Rod.

Did you hear about the hotel owner being robbed?
Police held an Inn-quest.

The earthquake meeting was canceled after a motion
from the floor.

Did you hear the joke about the church bell? It's never
been tolled.

Lost my job at the orange juice factory. Turns out I
couldn't concentrate.

Dad: I gave your brother a pack of baseball
cards.

Kid: He's only one! He can't read.

Dad: That's okay, he can look at the pitchers.

What do you call a surgeon with eight arms?
A Doc-topus.

What do you get when you cross a flower with a flying insect?
A forget-me-gnat.

RANDOM THOUGHTS

I'm so good at sleeping, I can do
it with my eyes closed.

That cemetery looks overcrowded.
People must be dying to get in there.

Never trust a deli sandwich.
They're too full of baloney.

I don't like it when people say that age
is only a number. It's clearly a word.

What do basketball players like on their burgers?
Swish cheese.

What do you get when you cross a peach with a pooch?
A pit bull.

What do you call a white bear that plays games on a horse?
A polo bear.

DAD QUOTE: My dad used to say you should fight fire with fire. Which is probably why he lost his job as a fireman.

What do you get when you cross a cat with an ice sculpture?
Frisky the Snowman.

Dad: Why are the baker's kids so bored?
Son: Please, Dad, don't . . .
Dad: They got muffin to do.

Dad: Don't throw that plastic bag into the Louisiana swamp!
Daughter: Why not, Dad?
Dad: 'Cause it's not bayou degradable.

Why did the kangaroo cancel his health insurance policy?
He was tired of paying out-of-pocket expenses.

Boss: How can you do so many dumb things in one day?
Dad: I get up early.

I just took a picture of a wheat field. It came out a little grainy.

Kid: Who was that, Dad?

Dad: Oh, it was a policeman.

Kid: What'd he want?

Dad: He wanted to know where I was between five and six.

Kid: What'd you tell him?

Dad: Kindergarten.

Where does Tiger Woods keep his boat?
The Golf of Mexico.

Where do cats live?
In apurrrtments.

Where do pigs live?
In trailer porks.

Where do cartoon dogs live?
In a Scooby-Doo-plex.

The only thing flat-earthers have to fear is sphere itself.

Dad: Did you hear about the new movie *Planet of the Ape-ricots*?
Son: Oh brother.
Dad: Yeah, it's rated peachy-13.

What do they have for breakfast in earthquake zones?
Panquakes.

DAD QUOTE: Finland just closed their borders. That's right, no one will ever cross the Finnish line.

What's brown and not too heavy?
Light brown.

What kind of doctor is Dr. Pepper?
A fizzician.

I'm reading a book about the history of glue. I can't put it down.

Why aren't people happy on the weekend?
'Cause one of the days is sadder day.

RANDOM THOUGHTS

I'm thinking about an all-almond diet, but that's just nuts.

Saw a baguette at the zoo. It was bread in captivity.

I'm staying outside, so if anyone asks, just tell them I'm out standing.

If you get an email about canned meat, don't open it. It's Spam.

Teenager: I'm tan from the sun.

Dad: Hi, Tan. I'm Dad from the earth.

Your mom told me to buy a telescope since I'm so into astronomy. I told her I'd look into it.

Mom says I have two faults: I don't listen and something else.

Spent $100 on a new belt and it doesn't even fit. What a huge waist.

Or better yet, let me give you my cell number.

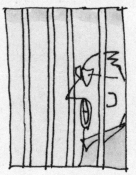

Dad: I could never be a plumber.

Son: Why not?

Dad: I can't imagine watching your entire life's work go down the drain.

What did the band leader name his twin daughters?
Anna One, Anna Two . . .

Did you hear about the guy who was caught stealing a barbecue? The cops really grilled him.

What goes down but never comes up?
A yo.

What did the pirate get on his report card?
Seven C's.

What's the difference between a tennis ball and the Prince of Wales?
One is thrown in the air, and the other is heir to the throne.

DAD QUOTE: Went to buy some camouflage pants this morning but couldn't find any.

Son: Can I borrow a bookmark?
Dad: Sure, but my name is Brian.

Where do birds invest their money?
The stork market.

How did the monkey like his lunch?
He went bananas.

I lost another audiobook. Now I'll never hear the end of it.

Where do cats wait to pay their bills?
In the fee line.

Mom: Honey, if you don't stop snoring, I'm going to toss you out on your ear!

Dad: Does it really bother you that much?

Mom: Not just me, the entire congregation!

What did Tennessee? The same thing Arkansas.

You know who was faster than Bruce Lee? His brother Sudden.

What do you call James Bond taking a bath?
Bubble O Seven.

RANDOM THOUGHTS

Good news! I finished my 14-day
diet in just 3 hours!

Just read a book about falling down
stairs. It's a step-by-step guide.

Just found out I'm color-blind. The diagnosis
came completely out of the purple.

Kid: Dad, is this safe to eat?

Dad: No, son, it's for storing our valuables.

The guy who plays the triangle in our band is leaving. Thanks for every ting.

I gave my handyman a list of things I needed him to do, but he only did numbers 1, 3, and 5. Turns out he only does odd jobs.

Dad: Why did the small pepper put on a sweater?

Daughter: Please, Dad, no . . .

Dad: He was a little chili.

If you boil your funny bone, does that make it a laughingstock? Thought that was humerus.

What's the fastest liquid in the world?
Milk! It's pasteurized before you can even see it!

Mom asked me if I'd seen the dog bowl. I said, "I didn't know he could."

What does a baby computer call its father?
Data!

DAD QUOTE: Sometimes I tuck my knees into my chest and lean forward. That's how I roll!

I took care of rabbits for a while, but I quit 'cause I got scared. It was a hare-raising experience.

I'm only familiar with 25 letters in the alphabet. I don't know why.

They recently discovered a 2,000-year-old oil stain. It's from ancient Greece.

How do you watch a fly-fishing tournament?
You livestream it.

You know how to tell the difference between an alligator and a crocodile? You'll see one later and one in a while.

What do you call 50 pigs and 50 deer?
A hundred sows and bucks.

A woman walks into a nice restaurant and speaks to the maître d'.

Maître d': Do you have reservations?

Diner: No, I'm confident I want to eat here.

I just got back from a protest in support of John Deere. You could say I'm protractor.

Why did the raisin go out with the prune?
'Cause he couldn't find a date.

I'm working on inventing a pencil with an eraser on both ends. But, hmmm, I just don't see the point.

My dad used to say, "Don't worry, it could be worse. I mean, you could be stuck underground in a hole filled with water." I know he meant well.

I got fired from my job in the kitchen for stealing utensils. It was a whisk I was willing to take.

Kid: Dad, I want to become an archaeologist.

Dad: No, son, I don't want to see your life in ruins.

Why did the football coach hit the vending machine?
He wanted to get his quarterback.

DAD QUOTE: I love elevator jokes. They work on so many levels.

How do lawyers say goodbye?
"I'll be suing you!"

What state has the most streets?
Rhode Island.

Did you hear that the Terminator retired? Guess he's the Exterminator now.

Dogs can't operate MRI machines. But CAT scan.

I told my doctor I keep hearing a buzzing. He said it's just a bug going around.

What kind of car does a sheep like to drive?
A Lamb-orghini.

When the two pieces of bread met, it was loaf at first sight.

I didn't like working as an IRS accountant. The job was too taxing.

DAD QUOTE: Dads tell really bad jokes because they want you to become a *groan* up.

Dad: When I worked as a lumberjack, I cut down exactly 2,346 trees.

Kid: Wow! How do you know that?

Dad: Every time I cut one down, I kept a log.

RANDOM THOUGHTS

If we're a country committed to free speech, why are there phone bills?

If FedEx and UPS merged, would they be called Fed Up?

I never buy preshredded cheese. Doing it yourself is grate.

Is it okay to use my AM radio after noon?

Do you know how to build a pyramid?

Well, yeah. Up to a point.

What's the world's largest punctuation mark?
The 100-yard dash.

What's a monkey's favorite Christmas song?
"Jungle Bells."

How do moths swim?
They use the butterfly stroke.

I got really mad at my friend Mark for stealing my dictionary. I said, "Mark, my words!"

Did you hear about the dating site in Prague? It's called Czech-mate.

My pillow fell off the bed and hit the floor really hard. You think it might have a con-cushion?

The motel tried to charge me 10 extra dollars for air conditioning. I told them that wasn't cool.

What do college professors snack on?
Academia nuts.

Did you hear about the guy who swallowed a dictionary? He didn't breathe a word of it to anyone.

What do you call a cat who lives in an igloo?
An Eski-mew.

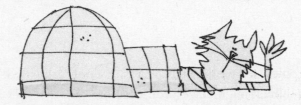

Dad: Why did the cannonball lose its job?
Daughter: Don't, Dad, don't!
Dad: It got fired.

DAD QUOTE: My teachers all told me I'd never amount to anything because I procrastinate so much. I told them, "Just you wait!"

Dad: Why did they call them the Dark Ages?
Son: Please, no, Dad.
Dad: 'Cause there were so many knights!

Did you hear about the explosion in the French cheese factory? There was de Brie everywhere.

I got a new job as the head of Old MacDonald's farm. I'm the C-I-E-I-O.

Somebody broke in and stole my coffee, my sunlamp, and my parrot. I don't know how they sleep at night.

What do you get from a pampered cow?
Spoiled milk.

What do you call a musician with problems?
A trebled man.

What happened when a faucet, a tomato, and some lettuce were in a race?
The lettuce was a head, the faucet was running, and the tomato was trying to ketchup.

DAD QUOTE: People think *icy* is the easiest word to spell. Come to think of it, I see why.

What's the best way to get straight A's?
Use a ruler.

Want to hear a roof joke? It might be over your head, but the first one's on the house.

A man walks into a library and asks the librarian for books on paranoia. She whispers, "They're right behind you."

A cement mixer and a prison bus crashed on the highway. Police are warning citizens to be on the lookout for a group of hardened criminals.

DAD QUOTE: I saw a movie about how ships are put together. It was riveting.

I quit my job at the coffee shop yesterday. It was the same old grind, over and over.

Did you hear about the janitors who went up into space? At the last minute, they had to scrub the mission.

What kind of music do astronauts listen to?
Nep-tunes.

DAD QUOTE: I had a neck brace put on 10 years ago, and I haven't looked back since.

Patient: Doctor, you've got to help me! I'm convinced I'm a needle and thread!
Doctor: How do you feel?
Patient: Sew-sew.

What steals your stuff while you're in the bathtub?
A robber ducky.

DAD QUOTE: Whenever I'm putting the car in reverse, I think, *Ah, this takes me back.*

A storm blew off 25 percent of my roof last night. Oof.

Your mom accused me of having zero empathy. I can't understand how she can feel that way.

My kid is obsessed with counting, so I sent him to his room. I wonder what he's up to now.

It's hard to explain puns to a kleptomaniac because they always take things literally.

Kid: Is this pool safe for diving?

Dad: It deep ends.

Why did you bring your sketchbook to bed?

I wanted to draw the curtains.

Dad: I'm reading some books on plants.

Mom: Botany?

Dad: No, I got them from the library.

Patient: Doctor, I'm convinced I'm a toll bridge!

Doctor: Oh my. What's come over you?

Patient: So far, two trucks and a bus.

I can watch the sunrise from my bedroom.

So what? From my family room, I can watch the kitchen sink.

Why don't anteaters ever get sick?

'Cause they have all those little antibodies inside them.

Teacher: If you have five dollars and you ask your father for five more, how much money will you have?

Student: Five dollars.

Teacher: Boy, you don't know your math.

Student: You don't know my father.

Daughter: Dad, have your eyes been checked lately?

Dad: No, they've always been solid brown.

DAD QUOTE: I'm so diligent that last week I stayed up all night studying for a blood test.

Son: Dad, may I join the track team?

Dad: Run that by me again.

Dad: Excuse me, how much is a room?

Hotel Clerk: $150 a night.

Dad: Do you take children?

Hotel Clerk: Nope. Just cash or credit cards.

I'm so broke I can't even pay attention!

Where do TVs go on vacation?
To remote places.

I get carried away sometimes. Usually because I refuse to leave!

What do you call a guy lying on your front step?
Matt.

What do they call the time in history when nerds ruled the land?
The Dork Ages.

Teacher: Okay, Jimmy, be honest. Your parents helped you with your homework, right?

Jimmy: No, they did it all by themselves!

So, if you carry the two...

No, that's not right.
Try adding the seven...

A woman walks into a shop and says, "I think I need a stronger prescription for my glasses."

The guy behind the counter says, "I'll say! This is a bakery."

I just saw a guy spill all his Scrabble letters on the road. I asked him, "What's the word on the street?"

Dad: What did the tin man say when he got run
over by a steamroller?

Daughter: It's okay, Dad. We don't want to know.

Dad: "Curses! Foil again!"

I'm thinking of moving to Moscow. But there's no point
in Russian into things.

I'm new around here.

RANDOM THOUGHTS

Turning vegan would be a big missed steak.

Bye, bye, boiling water. You will be mist.

Be nice to your dentist.
After all, he has fillings too.

What do you do when someone's been injured in a peekaboo accident?
Take them to the ICU.

Why did the police officer cry while he was writing a ticket?
It was a moving violation.

What's one thing you'll get on your birthday, guaranteed?
A year older.

DAD QUOTE: I'd grow my own food if only I could find bacon seeds.

What do you say to a rabbit on its birthday?
"Hoppy birthday."

Why don't pirates shower before they walk the plank?
Because they'll just wash up on shore later.

What do you call a banker in the Old West who set up loans for people?
The Loan Arranger.

> **Dad:** What's the key to a great Thanksgiving
>   dinner?
> **Kid:** Dad, don't.
> **Dad:** The tur-key.

Just failed my karate exam. I could kick myself.

What did the broccoli say to the celery?
"Quit stalking me!"

I joined a support group for compulsive talkers. It's called On and On Anon.

Dad: What did one egg say to the other one?
Daughter: Please, Dad.
Dad: "The yolk's on you!"
Daughter: Oh, dear.
Dad: Thought that would crack you up.

Dad: I can tell that bike is quite a thinker.
Son: Why is that?
Dad: I can see the wheels turning.

Why is it so windy inside a stadium?
Because there are thousands of fans inside.

How much does a pirate pay for corn?
A buck an ear.

DAD QUOTE: I'd like to thank all the sidewalks for keeping me off the streets.

People tell me my job as a waiter isn't very good. But, hey, it puts food on the table.

What kind of tree can you carry in one hand?
A palm tree.

What did one DNA strand say to the other?
"Do these genes make me look fat?"

Two antennas met, fell in love, and got married. The ceremony wasn't much, but the reception was excellent.

Why can't the music teacher start his car?
His keys are on the piano.

DAD QUOTE: Yesterday I spent 20 minutes fixing a broken clock. At least I *thought* it was 20 minutes.

Where does Superman's wife drive?
In the Lois Lane.

Why do Scottish people always have plumbing issues?
'Cause they only have bagpipes.

DAD QUOTE: I used to be addicted to the Hokey Pokey. But then I turned myself around.

What do you call a kid who doesn't like math class?
A calcu-hater.

Where should a dog never go shopping?
A flea market.

What do planets like to read?
Comet books.

> **Kid:** My dad's a realtor, and he's really strong.
> **Friend:** Really?
> **Kid:** Yeah, he can flip a house all by himself.

Why do space rocks taste better than earth rocks?
They're a little meteor.

Why did ancient Egyptians shave their heads?
To be more pharaoh-dynamic.

DAD QUOTE: For so long, I couldn't remember how to throw a boomerang. But then it came back to me.

She lost her job at the hot dog stand for putting her hair in a bun.

She loved the pastry chef but always feared he'd dessert her.

Dad: Do you want to hear a joke backward?

Kid: Sure.

Dad: Okay, start laughing.

Financially, I'm set for life. Provided I never buy anything ever again.

What do people like to wear in England?
Tea-shirts.

What has six feet and sings?
A musical trio.

DAD QUOTE: I saw a sign that said, "Watch for Children," and I thought that sounded like a fair trade.

Why did the sesame seed keep telling jokes?
It was on a roll.

Why did the guy start selling yeast?
He wanted to raise some dough.

What do you call a baby monkey?
A chimp off the old block.

How do dinosaurs pay their bills?
With tyrannosaurus checks.

Dad: What happens when you touch a window?
Son: I don't know. What?
Dad: You feel the pane.

DAD QUOTE: My kid dropped the entire basket of laundry right in front of me, and I just stood there. I watched it all unfold.

I never trust atoms. They make up everything.

What do you call a lazy doctor?
Dr. Do Little.

I don't play soccer because I enjoy the sport. I'm just doing it for kicks.

DAD QUOTE: I used to be a narcissist. But now look at me.

What do you call George Washington's false teeth?
Presidentures.

I told my contractor not to carpet my steps. He gave me a blank stair.

Doctor: Sorry about keeping you waiting.
Dad: No problem. I'm patient.

Dad: I can cut this log in two just by staring at it.
Kid: That's impossible!
Dad: I know; I didn't believe it either, but I saw it with my own two eyes.

Why do you have all those
    leaves in your car?

It's my Autumn-mobile.

A guy is walking on the beach when he trips over a genie's lamp. He rubs it, and the genie appears.

Genie: What's your first wish?

Guy: I want to be rich.

Genie: Okay, Rich, what's your second wish?

Optometrist: Your results aren't very good.

Man: Can I see them?

Optometrist: Probably not.

Kid: Thanks for the ride. I'll call you later.

Dad: Don't call me Later; call me Dad.

Woman: Doc, will I be able to play the piano after this surgery?

Doctor: Yes, you'll be fine.

Woman: Great! I've always wanted to play a musical instrument.

I really don't like my ancient Middle Eastern history class. The teacher tends to Babylon.

Guy: That puppet show was great! Were you involved?

Dad: Yeah, I had a hand in it.

I had plans to research sinkholes, but they fell through.

My friend thanked me for buying him an elephant for his room. I said, "Don't mention it."

Orion's Belt is just a waist of space.

RANDOM THOUGHTS

Did you hear how all the furry aquatic animals escaped from the aquarium? It was otter chaos.

A ship carrying red paint collided with a ship carrying purple paint. Both crews have been marooned.

I can't believe I got fired from the clock factory. After all the extra hours I put in!

DAD QUOTE: When I was little, my dad told me I could be anybody I wanted to be. Turns out this is called identity theft.

Where do rabbits go after their wedding?
On their bunnymoon.

Our neighborhood baker stopped making donuts. He said he got tired of the hole thing.

DAD QUOTE: I decided to do more reading this year, so I put subtitles on my TV.

Ah, all my winter fat is gone. Now I have spring rolls.

DAD QUOTE: A well-balanced diet . . . is a burger in each hand.

What did the counselor say to the sandpaper?
"Don't be so rough on yourself."

Kleptomaniacs think the best things in life are free.

Why was the teacher upset with the Xerox machine?
She caught it copying someone else's paper.

DAD QUOTE: The four seasons are all different.
Summer warmer than others.

What's the best snack to eat during a scary movie?
Ice cream!

I tried running a dating site for chickens. But it was hard
making hens meet.

Kid: Can I have a loan?

Dad: No, son. Money doesn't grow on trees, you know.

Kid: So then why do banks have branches?

Dad: Don't laugh too loud in Hawaii.

Kid: Why not?

Dad: They just want a low ha.

Did you hear about the population of Ireland? It's Dublin.

Why did the cell phone need glasses?

It lost its contacts.

I sold my vacuum cleaner the other day. All it was doing was collecting dust.

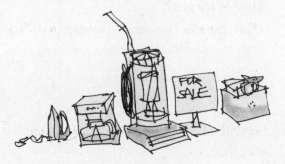

DAD QUOTE: I'm a really down-to-earth guy because of . . . you know, gravity.

I asked my date to meet me at the gym, but she never showed up. Guess the two of us aren't going to work out.

If you take your watch to get fixed, don't pay the guy before. Wait till the time is right.

Dad: Hey, kids, I want to teach you the easiest dance on earth.

Kids: What is it?

Dad: The elevator dance. No steps.

Good news! The LEGO Store has opened! People are lined up for blocks.

Mom: Why do you keep burping?

Dad: I had belchin' waffles for breakfast.

Kid: What time is it?

Dad: Ten to.

Kid: Ten to what?

Dad: Ten to your own business.

Within minutes, the detectives knew what the murder weapon was—it was a brief case.

DAD QUOTE: Always give 100 percent. Unless you're donating blood.

Kid: Dad, are we pyromaniacs?
Dad: Yes, we arson.

I remember the first time I saw a universal remote control. I thought to myself, *Now this changes everything.*

Good thing I don't have to hunt for food. I don't even know where tacos live.

I slept like a log last night. Woke up in the fireplace.

Why did the cow cross the road?
To get to the udder side.

Mom keeps telling me to stop acting like butter. But I'm on a roll now.

My kid's really upset 'cause he says I'm too obsessed with astronomy. What planet is he on?

DAD QUOTE: Say what you want about Captain Hook, but he ran that entire pirating operation single-handedly.

I used to get little shocks when I touched metal objects, but recently that stopped. Needless to say, I'm ex-static.

My son wants to study burrowing rodents. I told him to gopher it.

Dad: If you had tea with the Queen, what kind of tea would it be?

Daughter: I don't want to know.

Dad: Royal-tea.

Dad: Where do dentists go on vacation?

Son: No, please!

Dad: Floss Vegas.

RANDOM THOUGHTS

Water is heavier than butane because
butane is a lighter fluid.

I probably should go on a diet, but I've
got too much on my plate already.

I would love to get paid to sleep.
Talk about a dream job!

What do you do when a sink is knocking on your door?
You let that sink in.

I was sitting in traffic the other day. Then an officer made me stand up and move to the sidewalk.

Dad: I really hurt myself at the seafood
restaurant last week.

Son: What happened?

Dad: I think I pulled a mussel.

I'm so insecure I once painted a self-portrait of someone
else.

What's made of leather and sounds like a sneeze?
A shoe.

I find it suspicious that you're only sick on weekdays.

It must be my weekend immune system.

Where does an astronaut park the space shuttle?
At a parking meteor.

How did the giraffe do in his classes?
He got high honors.

RANDOM THOUGHTS

I'm just itching to tell you about my allergies.

I used to think I was indecisive.
Now I'm not so sure.

What if soy milk is just regular milk
introducing itself in Spanish?

If a parsley farmer is sued,
do they garnish his wages?

Haven't sold a single copy of my autobiography. That's the story of my life.

What did you find when you traced your family tree? Termites.

DAD QUOTE: I hate jokes about student debt. They never pay off.

This bike in the neighborhood keeps running me over. It's a vicious cycle.

I asked the surgeon if I could administer my own anesthetic. He said, "Go ahead, knock yourself out."

My daughter told me she saw a deer on the way to school. I said, "How did you know where it was going?"

What do you call a teenager who never grows up?
Constantine.

Where do sharks go on vacation?
Finland.

People are usually shocked when they find out I'm not a very good electrician.

Where do dads store their dad jokes?
In a dad-a-base.

What does a Slovakian sound engineer say?
"Czech one two . . . Czech one two . . ."

Why was the mother firefly unhappy?
'Cause her kids weren't very bright.

RANDOM THOUGHTS

A bald man got a deal on a new wig. Only a dollar! It was a small price toupee.

As soon as you find out someone has 10,000 bees, marry them. That's when you know they're a keeper.

The CEO of IKEA was just elected president of Sweden. He should have his cabinet put together by the end of the week.

The butcher couldn't reach the meat on the top shelf. The steaks were too high.

How do pickles enjoy the weekend?
They relish it.

Son: Did you see that cop dressed as a pilot?
Dad: Yeah, I guess he's a plane-clothes officer.

Teacher: Nick, who invented fractions?

Nick: Was it Henry the ⅛?

Dad: Did you know there's a city where
everyone has the same blood type?

Kid: Please, Dad, no.

Dad: It's Taipei.

Tourist: What's the fastest way to get downtown?

Local: Are you walking or driving?

Tourist: Driving.

Local: That's the fastest way.

Nurse, why did you bring
that red pen to work?

In case I need to draw blood.

When your mom told me to stop acting like a flamingo, that's when I put my foot down.

What did the beaver say to the tree?
"It's been nice gnawing you."

Tourist: How can you tell that's a dogwood tree?
Ranger: I can tell by its bark.

Where do bad rainbows go?
Prism. But don't worry, it's a light sentence.

I switched the labels in my wife's spice cabinet. She hasn't noticed yet, but the thyme is cumin.

I have a phobia of German sausage. I fear the wurst.

The invisible man married the invisible woman. Their kids aren't much to look at either.

Daughter: Dad, can you tell me where the English Channel is?

Dad: I can't, we don't have cable.

Where do fish keep their money?
In the riverbank.

I'm taking my crayons to the zoo. I want to try coloring outside the lions.

What do you call a flower that runs on electricity?
A power plant.

Dad: Did you hear about the bedbug that was expecting?

Kid: Don't say it.

Dad: Yeah, she's going to have her baby in the spring.

How do astronauts keep clean?
They take meteor showers.

DAD QUOTE: Last night, I dreamed I was a car muffler. I woke up exhausted.

To the person who stole my place in line: I'm after you now.

I wouldn't say my house has the best ceiling in the world, but it's up there.

What kind of car does Mickey Mouse's girlfriend drive?
A Minnie van.

Where do cows buy their clothes?
From cattle-logs.

RANDOM THOUGHTS

I entered the suntan Olympics,
but I only got bronze.

Milk is good, but it could be butter.

I started a boating business in my attic.
The sails are going through the roof.

A store owner fought off a robber using
only his labeling gun. Police are now looking
for a man with a price on his head.

I keep dreaming I'm in a clothes dryer. I toss and turn all night.

Dad: The ducks at the park keep trying to bite our dog.

Kid: Why?

Dad: He's a pure bread.

I was living on a houseboat when I fell in love with the girl next door. Sadly, we began to drift apart.

Why does a grape make a great mom?
Because she loves raisin' children.

What do you get if a hen lays an egg on the top of a hill?
Eggrolls.

Mom: Why do you have that rubber band around your head?
Dad: I'm trying to make snap decisions.

What do you call an average ancient Greek?
Mediocrities.

What fish performs operations at the fish clinic?
The sturgeon.

I'm going to become a candlemaker. It's so easy. They only work on wick ends.

How can you make sure you never wake up sleepy and grumpy?
Just don't have a sleepover with the seven dwarfs.

What did the hamburger name his daughter?
Patty.

What do Alexander the Great and Winnie the Pooh have in common?

Same middle name.

I couldn't believe it when the highway department called my dad a thief. But when I got home, all the signs were there.

Why is England so wet?

Because the Queen has reigned there for years.

RANDOM THOUGHTS

Did you hear about the corduroy pillows? They're making headlines.

The world tongue-twister champion just got arrested. I hear they're going to give him a really tough sentence.

I really wanted to become a monk. But I never got the chants.

Patient: Doctor, you've got to help me! I'm convinced I'm a cocker spaniel!

Psychiatrist: Come in and lie down on the couch.

Patient: I can't! I'm not allowed on the furniture!

My doctor told me to play 18 holes every day. So I took up the harmonica.

Did you hear about the missing barber? Police are combing the city.

Dad: I fell off a 30-foot ladder yesterday.
Friend: Wow! Are you okay?
Dad: Yeah, I was just on the second rung.

What did the lawyer name his daughter?
Sue.

Your mom said I need to stop making police-related puns. I said, "Okay, I'll give it arrest."

A scientist crossed poison ivy with a four-leaf clover and got a rash of good luck.

I'm quitting my job as a personal trainer because the weights are too heavy. I just turned in my too-weak notice.

What do you get when you cross a rooster with a giraffe?
An animal that wakes people who live on the top floor.

Cock-a-doodle-do

I'm trying archery while wearing a blindfold.

In other words, you don't know what you're missing.

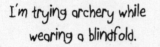

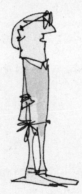

Your mom dated a clown before she met me. Needless to say, I had some pretty big shoes to fill.

Daughter: Dad, will you join me in a cup of soup?
    Dad: Do you think we can both fit?

    Dad: My wife and I are going to the Caribbean.
Neighbor: Jamaica?
    Dad: No, she wanted to go.

Anybody want my old copies of *Chiropractic Weekly*? I've got loads of back issues.

    Mom: Ever seen an eggroll?
    Dad: No, but I've seen an apple turnover.

What happens to a frog who overparks?

He gets toad.

Waiter: And how did you find your steak, sir?

Customer: Easy. I just moved the mashed potatoes and there it was!

What's green and brown and crawls through the grass?

A Girl Scout who's lost her cookie.

I worked for five years in an origami store until it folded.

Why are you putting that cake in the freezer?
The recipe says to ice it after baking.

I went on a once-in-a-lifetime vacation—never again.

Diner: Will the band play anything I ask them to?
Band Leader: Sure.
Diner: Then ask them to play chess.

Boss: What were you before you started working here?
Employee: Happy.

Salesman: This computer will do half your work for you.

Dad: Great, I'll take two.

DAD QUOTE: My son just bought a reversible jacket. I can't wait to see how it turns out.

Dad: Do I need to put these stamps on myself?

Postal Worker: Well, most people put them on the envelope.

I was confused when the only gift I got for my birthday was a bucket of Play-Doh. I didn't know what to make of it.

Kid: My dad is a magician. He saws people in half.

Friend: Do you have any siblings?

Kid: Three half sisters and a half brother.

Sunday School Teacher: In the Bible, Lot was told to take his wife and flee out of the city. His wife looked back and turned to salt.

Child: What happened to the flea?

Why did the baby cookie cry?
Because his father was a wafer so long.

I just watched a cool movie on Donald and Daisy Duck. It was a duckumentary.

Dad: Did you hear that Max got a job as a ditch digger?

Son: Really? How did that happen?

Dad: He just fell into it.

Kyle stole the ketchup, but the cops caught him red-handed.

What do you call an alligator with a law degree?
A litigator.

Objection, Your Honor!

Dad: Hey, honey, what do you say to a nice walk?

Mom: That sounds great.

Dad: Good, will you pick me up some donuts and chips while you're out there?

According to statistics, a person is robbed in Chicago every seven minutes.

That poor guy should consider moving.

There's a group of people out there who refuse to use coins.

Wow, sounds like a lot of non-cents to me.

What did the elevator say to the other elevator?

"I think I'm coming down with something."

What do you call a snake who works for the government?
A civil serpent.

That's the seventh passenger today who's told me I'm a terrible bus driver. I don't know where these people get off.

Mom asked me to put ketchup on the shopping list. I did and now I can't read any of it.

Dad: It's times like this I wish I'd listened to what my dad always said.

Mom: What was that?

Dad: I don't know; I wasn't listening.

DAD QUOTE: The doctor told me I was going deaf. That was hard news to hear.

Kid: My new radio is so powerful that last night I got Mexico.

Dad: Big deal. Last night I just opened my window and got chilly.

What do you call a paper airplane that doesn't fly?
Stationery.

Say, Doctor, would you mind
if I sewed up my own incision?

Go ahead, suture self.

Never yell through a colander. You might strain your voice.

Customer: Will my pizza be long?
   Worker: No, it'll be round just like all the other ones.

   Dad: I'm voting for Mr. Goodbar this November.
   Kid: How come?
   Dad: 'Cause he's the best candy-date.

How many psychologists does it take to change a light bulb?

Only one, but the light bulb really has to want to change.

RANDOM THOUGHTS

So what if I don't know what the word *apocalypse* means? It's not like it's the end of the world.

I quit my job as a treadmill tester.
Just felt like I wasn't going anywhere.

Nowadays, the name Lance is unusual. But in medieval times, people were called Lance a lot.

Why is the math book so sad?
Because it's got so many problems.

I'd like to get a job cleaning mirrors. It's really something I could see myself doing.

What does a clock do when it's hungry?
It goes back four seconds.

Our town was so small its zip code was a fraction.

If I had 50 cents for every math test I failed, I'd have
$7.40.

I burnt my Hawaiian pizza. I guess I should have put it
on aloha temperature.

Did you know you can actually hear the blood in your veins?

You just have to listen varicosely.

I broke my finger last week. On the other hand, I'm okay.

What did the duck say when he bought some lip balm?

"Just put it on my bill."

Why did the mummy not go on vacation?

He was afraid he'd relax and unwind.

What do you get when you cross cocoa with a herd of cows?

Chocolate moos.

Why didn't the chili take up archery?
He didn't habanero.

I'm not very good at rock collecting, but I'm picking it up as I go along.

It doesn't matter if you're rich or poor. At the end of the day . . . it's night.

Who invented the telephone and carries your luggage?
Alexander Graham Bellhop.

Doctor, you've got to help me! I'm convinced I'm a deck of cards!

Have a seat. I'll deal with you in a minute.

What do you call it when you finish your tea?

Tea end!

Why did the physics teacher break up with the biology teacher?

There was just no chemistry.

Why can't you ever borrow money from a leprechaun?

'Cause they're always a little short.

What's black and white and red all over?

A panda eating chili without utensils.

I'm setting up a hide-and-seek tournament, but good players are hard to find.

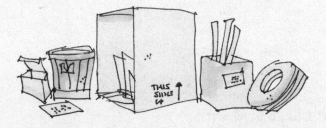

My wife was upset when I brought home a revolving chair, but then she sat on it. I think she's coming around.

My brother isn't too bright. Last week during a power failure at the mall, he got stuck on an escalator for two and a half hours.

Backward Jokes

Backward jokes give you the answer first, then the question. Here's an example:

The answer: SUPERVISOR
The question: What does Superman wear to keep the sun out of his eyes?

DESPAIR
What are you glad you have in case of a flat tire?

BURGLARIZE
What does a crook see through?

AVOIDABLE
What does a bullfighter try to do?

KITTY LITTER
What does Garfield throw out the car window?

COUNTERFEITER
What do you call a guy who puts kitchen cabinets together?

DESCENT

What's the difference between a cat and a skunk?

PARASITES

What do you see from the Eiffel Tower?

PARADOX

What do you call two physicians walking down the hall?

LAUGHINGSTOCK

What do you call cows with a good sense of humor?

HOGWASH

What's another name for a pig's laundry?

DR PEPPER

Who married Nurse Salt?

NUTELLA

What do you call the most recent hire at the bank?

MODEM

What did the gardener do to the lawns?

Need any help?

PHARMACIST

What's another name for a
helper on a farm?

EXTREME

What do you call a dry riverbed?

ANNOUNCE

What's $\frac{1}{16}$ of a pound?

AUTOBIOGRAPHY

What do you call the history of a car?

KNAPSACK

What do you call a sleeping bag?

Sandy Silverthorne, author of *Crack Yourself Up Jokes for Kids, More Crack Yourself Up Jokes for Kids, Made You Laugh!,* and *Now That's Funny,* has been writing and illustrating books since 1988 and currently has over 800,000 copies in print. His award-winning Great Bible Adventure children's series with Harvest House sold over 170,000 copies and has been distributed in eight languages worldwide. His One-Minute Mysteries series has sold over 240,000 copies. He's written and illustrated over 30 books and has worked with such diverse clients as Universal Studios Tour, Doubleday Publishers, Penguin, World Vision, the University of Oregon, the Charlotte Hornets, and the Academy of Television Arts and Sciences. Sandy has worked as a cartoonist, author, illustrator, actor, pastor, speaker, and comedian. Apparently, it's hard for him to focus. Connect with him at sandysilverthornebooks.com.

More Jokes for Kids from Sandy

Learn More about
SANDY

Head to **sandysilverthornebooks.com**
for jokes, Bible stories and lessons,
drawing tutorials, and more!
